BRITAIN IN OLD I

LANCING AND SOMPTING

PHILIP FRY

ALAN SUTTON PUBLISHING LIMITED

Alan Sutton Publishing Limited
Phoenix Mill · Far Thrupp · Stroud
Gloucestershire · GL5 2BU

First published 1995

Cover photographs: front: Lancing beach;
back: Hoe Court Farm, North Lancing.
Title page photograph: The National C. of E.
School, North Lancing.

British Library Cataloguing in Publication Data.
A catalogue record for this book is available from
the British Library.

ISBN 0-7509-0940-4

Typeset in 9/10 Sabon.
Typesetting and origination by
Alan Sutton Publishing Limited.
Printed in Great Britain by
WBC Limited, Bridgend.

This book is dedicated to my wife Caroline (Mo), and
our three dear sons Anthony, Mark and Stephen.

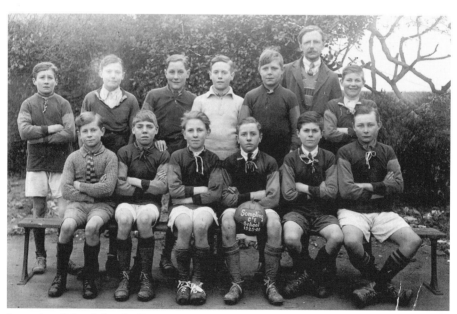

Sompting School football team, *c.* 1926. Back row, left to right: J. Etherington,
E. Miles, T. Bushby, S. Brown, F. Trussler, F. Archard, T. Coleman. Front row:
J. Duffield, R. Nye, B. Riddles, L. Burgess, J. Green, S. Knight.

Contents

Acknowledgements

While many of the photographs in this book are from my own collection, a lot have come from other people. I should like to express my warmest thanks to the following people who have contributed to this book by lending photographs and supplying information. Without them this book would not have been possible:

Members of my family: Derek, Albert, Elva, Eddie, Grace, Margaret and Clive (for his invaluable help with the computer). Hazel Trussler, Emily Wood, Joan Hunniball, Tom Coleman, Don Marshall, Malcolm Collins, John Mott, John Oxborough, Pete Matten, Johnny Grey, Mr and Mrs Last, Doreen and Roy Prior, Sheila and George Kirk, Mike Prince, Stan Hickman, Micky Stovell, Joyce Brown, Mrs Pennell.

Great care has been taken to ensure no copyright has been violated. If this has occurred, I apologize in advance and assure that it was not intentional. Errors will be corrected in any future editions.

The following publications have been useful in the preparation of this book:

Colebourne, Archie. *The Warren Heart Home;* Handford, B.W.T. *Lancing 1848–1930; Kellys Directories*, Worthing & District; Kerridge, R.G.P. *A History of Lancing; The Victoria County History of Sussex*

Introduction

Lancing and Sompting were small villages before the turn of the century. Both villages are mentioned in the Domesday Book of 1086, Sompting being linked with Cokeham, which later became part of it. The onslaught of development began in the 1920s. Only the lack of land has now slowed up this development, in Lancing at least. The only undeveloped land is to the east and far north of the parish. This expansion in Lancing increased the population immensely from approximately 2,000 in 1911 to approximately 18,500 in 1994, giving rise to the title of the largest village in England.

Three of the boundaries of Lancing are natural: the English Channel to the south, the Downs to the north, and the River Adur to the east. The fourth boundary, with Sompting, is Boundstone Lane. The old eponymous stone is kept at the Boundstone College in Sompting. The old Chichester to Brighton road, dating from Roman times, ran through the Lancing Manor grounds, continuing to the River Adur which it crossed at a point near to the old Sussex Pad public house.

There is a neolithic track at North Lancing that leads from the Sussex Pad Inn, past the seventeenth-century cottages at Hoe Court, up by Lancing Clump and on to Chanctonbury and Cissbury Rings. Articles, particularly pottery, from both the Pleistocene and Bronze Ages have been found at Lancing; some of these are now housed in the British Museum. In this same area, in 1828, a Romano-Celtic temple was unearthed and many coins and other antiquities were found.

In 1587 the people of Lancing, as in many coastal areas, made preparations to resist the Spanish Armada by setting up beacons on the headland to let others along the coast know whether the invasion had started. It is said that some of the timbers from the Spanish Armada wrecks were used in parts of Lancing's oldest house, 'The Old Cottage', which dates back originally to the thirteenth century. It is here that James II is reputed to have stayed on his way to Shoreham to take a ship to France.

The manor of Lancing was in the hands of the Goring family from the sixteenth century right up until 1827, when it was sold to James Martin Lloyd: he was at the time MP for Steyning. The Lloyd family retained the manor until the 1920s, when it was sold as plots of land for development, thus shaping the Lancing we know today. The manor house that stood in the grounds was demolished in 1972.

In about 1908, prior to the sale of the manor, the Lloyds sold a plot of land in South Lancing to the London, Brighton and South Coast Railway Company for the extension of its works, which at that time were situated in Brighton. Although originally manufacturing goods wagons, the works became the carriage works in about 1910. The news of this industry coming to Lancing was received with much opposition, as the village was still largely rural. The Brightonians who were transferred to work in Lancing were not too happy either, coming to a small village that had neither gas supply nor proper sanitation. Once the barriers were broken down, however, the carriage works became part of Lancing life and the largest employer in the village until they were closed in 1965.

Before the advent of the carriage works, Lancing's main industry had been its nurseries and market gardening, successful because of the rich soil between the Downs and the sea. The crops, which included fruit and flowers, were picked and sent up to London and surrounding towns. The glasshouses were still here albeit in depleted numbers until the late 1960s.

The earliest form of industry in Lancing was tourism, visitors coming to the area chiefly because of the then clean sea and the warm climate. The village was popular for bathing from the nineteenth century, although not in a grand way like neighbouring Brighton and Worthing, and the gentry of the time enjoyed staying at the terrace on the seafront.

The development of Sompting has been much less intense than that of Lancing; its population has risen from approximately 660 in 1911 to approximately 9,000 in 1994. Even today it continues to expand.

The village is bounded by four parishes: Lancing, Coombes, Findon and Broadwater. As at Lancing, the old Roman road from Chichester to Brighton ran through the village. It ran just south of St Mary's, the parish church, along the line now occupied by the bypass and on towards Lancing. At Park Brow there are remains of Bronze Age, Iron Age and Romano-British settlements. There is also a track crossing the southern slopes of Steepdown which most probably dates from the Iron Age.

Sompting and Cokeham were separate parishes up to the turn of the century and both had their own manor houses. The one at Cokeham has now gone and Sompting's manor house is part of Sompting Abbotts School. In the sixteenth century the manor was owned by Thomas Howard, the then Duke of Norfolk. In 1814 Sompting had a brush with royalty when Queen Caroline, consort of George IV, stayed at the manor house before travelling to Europe. In 1923 a Mrs Tristram owned the manor and she passed it to her son, Major Guy Tristram, who kept it until his death in 1963. Tristram Road in Sompting was named after the family.

From the middle of the nineteenth century a large area in Sompting was taken up by market gardens. The largest of these was owned by Mr Pullen-Burry until the late 1950s. One of his claims to fame was his moving greenhouse: it moved on wheels along brick tracks. Because of the mild climate on the south coast he could grow more exotic fruits like grapes, peaches and melons. Mr Pullen-Burry was the largest employer in Sompting, bringing in labour from Lancing as well. The nurseries in Sompting remained until the 1970s, but now, as in Lancing, market gardening is an industry of the past.

I hope you will enjoy looking at the last century of the lives and times of the two villages of Lancing and Sompting as much as I have enjoyed compiling this book.

Section One

SHOPS AND BUILDINGS

The Old Cottage, Mill Road, North Lancing, c. 1900. Parts of the cottage are

thought to date from the thirteenth century. In the 1950s a priest hole was

discovered in the attic which was used by priests during the reformation:

the entrance to the hole was up the chimney! The cottage was bought by James

Lloyd in 1796 and was part of the Lancing Manor Estate up until 1920.

It still stands today.

The Old Posting House, Mill Road, built *c.* 1580. The house was used as a stop for coaches and horses travelling between London and Portsmouth. The name has now been changed back to the original name of Grants Manor.

The Old Forge, Mill Road, 1940s. Parts of the Old Forge are reputed to date back to the early eighteenth century. It is now a private residence. Note the fine firebacks leaning up against the porch.

Malthouse Cottage, North Lancing, 1948. This was a tied cottage for the use of the workers of Malthouse Farm. It dates back to at least the eighteenth century.

Malthouse Cottage, c. 1950. The cottage still stands on the Old Shoreham Road, although it has lost much of its rural character, having had its thatch replaced with a tiled roof with dormer windows.

Malthouse Farmhouse, just along from Malthouse Cottage, *c.* 1910. The farmhouse dated back to the mid-eighteenth century. It was demolished in 1968 when the road was widened.

Old Tithe Barn, Mill Road, *c.* 1925. As the name implies the barn was used for storing the tithes. It was built at the beginning of the nineteenth century and was known then as Parsonage Barn. The McArthy family converted the barn into the guest house shown in the photograph; it was finally demolished in 1963 to make way for new housing.

The music room of the Old Tithe Barn Guest House, 1929.

Fircroft House, North Lancing, 1949. The house was built at the beginning of the nineteenth century. It was used as a guest house in the 1930s and remained so until the late 1950s, when it was demolished.

Culver Farmhouse, 1926. The house was occupied by the Penfold family of Sompting for the best part of the nineteenth century and it was this family, in 1882, which had the almshouses built opposite for the poor of Lancing. The farmhouse was demolished to make way for shops.

The Warren, Sompting Road, Lancing, 1940s. In 1927 the house was opened by Miss M. Booker and Miss Newton as a convalescent home for children. By 1930 it had become the Heart Home for Children, and had, at any given time, an average of seventy patients. In 1934 the home was renamed the Maud Booker Heart Home as a tribute to the founder. At the outbreak of the Second World War, The Warren was temporarily closed and the patients moved inland, to Cuckfield. After the war the patients returned to Lancing. The home was taken over by the National Health Service in 1948, but in 1950 the Ministry of Health closed it, deciding that it was too costly to run. A block of flats named Warren Court now stands on the site.

Littlecroft was an Edwardian-built terrace of agricultural cottages, shown here on the left. Demolished in 1963, the cottages were situated next to the almshouses in North Road. The Queensway shopping parade now stands on the site. Beneath part of the paved area of the parade is an old well, said to be still intact.

Yew Tree Cottages, South Lancing, 1906. The cottages were built in around 1800 and were situated in South Street opposite Penhill Road. They were destroyed by fire in 1957 (see pp. 89 and 90).

Ivy Cottages, East Street, South Lancing, 1920s. These cottages were built in around 1806 on an area of land called Horseshoe Field.

Coastguard Cottages, c. 1910. The cottages were erected in the early 1820s on the Lower Brighton Road, South Lancing. They were demolished in 1955 to make way for flats. On the beach can be seen the coastguards and their galley. E. Best was the officer in charge.

The Haven, Lower Brighton Road, South Lancing, opposite Kings Road, 1960s. From 1956 it was known as The Donkey Club Holiday Home. The Donkey Club was a charity which used to raise funds by running donkey Derbys at Wivelsfield Green, where the charity was born. Mr and Mrs Dinnage ran the home, which offered holidays to handicapped people. The Haven was demolished in the 1970s, to be replaced by a block of flats.

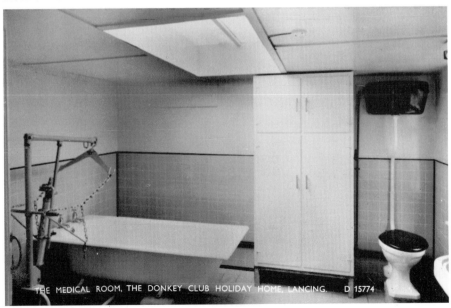

The medical room in The Donkey Club (The Haven), 1960s.

Colebourne & Co., on the corner of Penhill Road and South Street. This was a family grocer's and baker's shop. Mr Colebourne came to Lancing in 1870 and built the shop himself. When he died, at the age of 41, the shop stayed in the family and was passed on to one of his sons. The shop continued to thrive in the village for many years afterwards and is now owned by Gardener & Scardifields.

The bottom end of South Street, South Lancing, *c*. 1908. The little sweet shop on the corner was opened by Francis Trevett and he ran the business from 1842 until 1912. It was then passed on to May Trevett, seen here, who ran it with her sister Bessie until it closed in April 1961. It is now a fish and chip shop.

J.N. Last, chemist's, *c.* 1940. Mr Last came to Lancing in 1934 and started up his business in North Road by the level crossing. He later opened an optician's shop in Station Parade. The building shown here was built in around 1925.

Stocks House, West Street, Sompting, 1912. This house stood opposite The Marquis of Granby public house and was later demolished and replaced by a block of flats.

Myrtle Cottage, West Street, Sompting, 1912. The cottage is situated opposite Edwards Terrace. This view is looking north.

Sompting Abbotts, 1913. The original manor house of Sompting, this is a fine-looking building with Gothic architecture. It is now a private school. Note the unusual grazing animal!

Rectory House, West Street, Sompting, 1908. Built in the 1790s, this was later to be the home of the well-known market gardeners the Pullen-Burrys, who owned most of the surrounding land. Later, in the 1940s, it became a Roman Catholic convent school. It is now a rest home.

Rectory Lodge, West Street, Sompting, *c.* 1910.

Sompting general supply stores and post office, West Street, *c.* 1930. The shop at this time was owned and run by W. Atterbury; it is now a private house. Prior to this, the village post office was situated further up the street on the north side, in the front room of a cottage, next door to Trelawnys Cottage.

Section Two

BUNGALOW TOWN
AND BEACH

St Nicholas, one of the many buildings that formed Bungalow Town. These buildings were constructed from redundant railway carriages with roofs of corrugated iron. Development of the town started around 1890 and by about 1909 there were 260 bungalows stretching from Lancing through to Shoreham-by-Sea. Originally they were inhabited by people from the entertainment world but later they became weekend and holiday homes. At the beginning of the Second World War most-of the bungalows that were still standing were removed, the beach was cleared, and defences put up for the war effort.

The bungalows, in a view looking east, 1909.

Dar-es-Salaam, named after a coastal city in south-east Africa, 1913. Some of the occupants who lived in Bungalow Town were a source of great amusement to the people of Lancing and Shoreham, as they would walk about with hardly any, or no, clothes on!

This photograph, taken in 1911, clearly shows how elaborately designed and constructed some of the bungalows were. This bungalow, called Roy, was destroyed during the great storm of Easter 1913.

Victoria (right) and Royal (left) bungalows, 1911. The owner of this bungalow obviously feels that an Englishman's home is his castle. It has a very patriotic appearance, with the Union Jack flying. The photograph is taken from a postcard, the sender of which was celebrating the birth of a baby, who, along with mum, was doing fine!

Bungalow Town, 1909. This group looks very much like a party of entertainers, having scotch on the rocks! One of the railway carriages can be seen quite clearly, as part of the bungalow next door.

A follow-up to the previous photograph, the group now relaxing after their meal. Note the fine bird cage hanging in the porch.

Mon Repos, one of the larger bungalows, 1909.

Homeleigh. Note the unusual pet the woman is holding. It is a small monkey – perhaps also an entertainer!

Sea Walk, looking west to Worthing, 1909. To the right are the Coastguard Cottages. The huge winch is for hauling the coastguard galley up the beach (see p. 14).

On the beach in front of the Coastguard Cottages, 1908. The clothing, and lack of smiles, gives this family photograph rather a Victorian feel.

A lovely Edwardian scene, 1908. This looks very much like a family outing, complete with dog, who, like everybody else, was well aware of the camera.

The Terrace, *c.* 1910. One of the buildings, Jubilee House, was paid for by the Lancing Building Society. In 1822 it was sold at auction for the princely sum of £625. The Terrace is still standing and the buildings are privately owned.

Lancing Beach, showing the fishing fleet of the day, *c.* 1910. The crowd of onlookers suggests that they had had a good catch.

The gentleman standing in the middle of this scene, photographed in about 1912, is one of the McArthy family, who were the photographers in Lancing village from around 1908. Their superb photography has left us with so many tangible reminders of days gone by.

G. Mott, chauffeur and general handyman, 1919. Mr Mott is standing next to his employer's Renault car, in Lower Brighton Road.

Dons Cottage, 1919. Situated on the north side of Lower Brighton Road, this was the home of Mr and Mrs Mott while they were having a house built further along the road.

Bon Sante, a bungalow right on the foreshore, 1908. The bungalow just behind is The Cliff, shown on the opposite page. It is clear from this photograph how it got its name.

Bon Sante, 1911. What a difference three years can make! Totally revamped, Bon Sante now has a chimney stack, fencing all round, a new water butt and a nice new lawn!

The Cliff, *c.* 1920. Situated in Lower Brighton Road, like a lot of the bungalows on the seafront, The Cliff was often let. Evelyn Waugh, the novelist, used to rent it in the summer. One wonders if he penned any of his novels there.

On the beach looking west, 1907. Note the tents!

A beach scene from the early part of this century. Note the patriotic Union Jack flying. The building is now known as the Mermaid Café.

The Widewater at the eastern end of Lower Brighton Road, 1938. The gardens shown here were taken up, to be replaced by defences for the war effort. They were never replanted. The Widewater salt lagoon is now a protected area for birds and wildlife.

Section Three

SPORTS AND PASTIMES

The first season of Lancing Athletic Football Club, 1946–7. Back row, left to right:
J. Smith, L. Smith, S. Hickman, L. Bushby, C. Gatland, D. Wood, E. France,
A. Thorne, E. Houchin, W. Swallow, S. Stevens. Front row: L. Shepherd, R. Bowles,
C. Haite, R. Downing, D. Davies, E. Brooks, A. Bingham. When the club started out, it
played at Croshaw Recreation Ground, in Sompting, and what a season it was too! The
club won three cups: the Brighton League Division 1, the Brighton College Cup and the
Sussex Intermediate Cup. The club was the forerunner of the modern day Lancing FC,
which plays at Culver Road.

Sompting Football Club, 1922, with what must be an early supporters' club!

A successful season for Sompting FC, 1947/8. Back row, left to right: J. Skinner (sec.), L. Green, F. Render, W. Knibbs, J. Stoner, M. Stovell, D. Smith. Front row: K. Ives (vice-captain), J. Miles, V. Osbourne (captain), L. Beeston, M. Smythe. The club won the Charity Cup and the Croshaw Cup, and was the undefeated league champion. Just to the left of J. Skinner on the back row is part of the well-trodden path which actually ran across the pitch!

Lancing Boys Club, 1948. Back row, left to right: Mr Woolridge, Ken Monk, Rupert Hines, John Pickett, Albert Fry, Les Wigglesworth, John Booker, Harry Boiling, Colin McKeown, Mr Hooper. Front row: Brian Truebridge, Tony Simmonds, Terry Parker, Brian Mansbridge, Ralph Charles. The club used to play on the lower pitch at Lancing College.

Abbey Rovers FC, winners of the Worthing Charity Cup, 1954. Back row, left to right: Brian Gill, Ernie Golds, Kit Carson, Albert Fry, Frank Salter, Reg George, Reg Picknal, 'Spud' Baker. Second row: Cyril Picknal, Cyril Fry, Harry Boiling, Geoff Peck, Paul Aldridge, Brendan Kelly. Front row: Dennis Trevett, Terry Parker, Peter Hugget, Tony Pointer, Terry Freeman, Kevin Murphy. The club was formed in 1946 by the late Arthur Messer and named after Abbey Nurseries in Sompting. Its first ground was at Blacksmiths Field but later it moved to Croshaw Rec., and then to Monks Rec. at Lancing, where this photograph was taken. In the early 1970s, when the author played for the team, its name was changed to Lancing and Sompting Legion. It stayed as such until 1993 when it was changed again to Lancing United, the name by which it is still known today.

Sompting cricket team, early 1900s. Matches were played in the grounds of Sompting Abbotts. No protective head gear was worn then, just a flat cap!

A few members of Sompting Cricket Club, 1948. Left to right: Derek Mitchell, Cecil Mitchell, Harold Matthews, George Bushby, Albert Fry, Fred Render, Bill Sisley, Bob Steele, Cecil Lindfield. The club only practised at Sompting Abbotts at this time; all the games were played at Lancing Manor. This eventually led to the demise of the original Sompting CC, which went on to become Manor Cricket Club.

Lancing and Sompting Legion Club, Culver Road, *c.* 1920. A black and white minstrel troupe is on stage.

Early tourism: the Lancing Holiday Camp. The camp was situated in the area of Beach Green, South Lancing.

Miss Trevett's dancing class, 1937. Doreen Willard (now Prior), Hilda Atherfold and Ruth Scrace are some of the willing participants.

A Pullen-Burry's nursery staff outing, just about to leave from Sompting in their Southdown charabanc, 1920s.

Section Four

MANOR HOUSE AND PARKS

The manor house, Lancing. The house remained in the hands of the Lloyd family from the

time it was built in the early eighteenth century up to the time it was sold to Lancing

College in 1920. The lands of the manor were sold off in large plots which resulted in

North and South Lancing being truly joined together to form the Lancing we know today.

In 1935 the college sold the house and gardens to Worthing and Rural District Council.

The manor house was still owned by the council when it was demolished in 1972, even

after a long and hard campaign by the people of Lancing to save it. It is still sadly missed

by all who remember it. In its place now is the Leisure Centre.

The manor house and part of the gardens from the east side, *c.* 1950.

A nice view of the manor gardens, also known locally as the second manor, 1940s. This view looks north.

Grace Fry (now Rainford) by the sundial, now gone, in the gardens of the manor house, *c.* 1944.

The manor house, 1953. The unusually shaped auxiliary fire station was built for use in the war years. The two children playing are Harry Trussler Jnr and Christine Andrews.

Looking north-west across the manor park, *c.* 1950. In the distance can be seen the old cricket pavilion, which was burned down in the 1970s. A lot of the trees were destroyed by Dutch elm disease and by the 1987 hurricane.

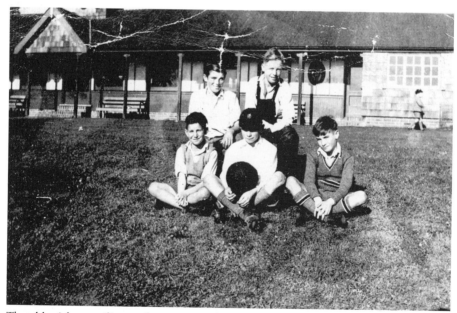

The old cricket pavilion at the manor park, 1944. The pavilion was constructed by C.F. Pycroft for use by parishioners. It was built around an old railway carriage called the Princess Helen. The team members are, back row, left to right: Albert Fry, Tony Ayling. Front row: Brian Mortimer, Tommy Boden, Bobby Cray.

Tennis at the manor, *c.* 1950. Left to right: Ralph Charles, Brian Mansbridge, Terry Parker, Mick Berry, Albert Fry, Ralph Batrick, Don Mansbridge, Roy Dibble, George Kirk. The two spectators in the background are Tony Simmonds and Jean Ames. The field in which they are sitting is now used for the allotments.

Manor Lodge, *c.* 1910. The lodge was at the entrance of the manor house grounds, at the top of Grinstead Lane, on the north side of the Old Shoreham Road. It was demolished in the early 1930s.

Manor Gardens, also known as Little Park, situated at the north-east corner of First Avenue and Eighth Avenue. It is said that the developer had built too many homes in the area and had to make amends by laying out a small park.

Monks Rec., Lancing, 1950s. Before the Second World War, there was a fine pair of ornate gates between the two brick piers. The low wall bordering the Rec. was also adorned with ornate railings. Like most iron work, these were melted down for the war effort.

Section Five

PARADES AND EVENTS

*An entrant in a Lancing carnival, Beach Green, c. 1930. John Upfield and Ted Charman
are driving the cart, which is being pulled by Colonel, who belonged to George Lisher. The
carnival used to start at the manor and parade through the village to Beach Green. It was
always a popular event in the village calendar, even during the author's childhood, but is
sadly no longer held.*

The Lancing carnival, 1926. The bicycle, along with the horse and cart, was more common than the car in the early part of the century. This one is totally adorned with butterflies and flowers. This photograph and the next one were taken outside a Victorian terrace called Cherry Tree Cottages in South Street. These cottages were demolished in 1970 to make way for a car park and flats.

Another entrant in the 1926 carnival. This one is called 'In Any Weather' and comes from the neighbouring harbour town of Shoreham-by-Sea, hence the seafaring topic.

Lancing Carriage Works Fire Brigade, with their horse-drawn manual fire engine, taking part in the carnival, 1938. Even the horses are posing!

Lancing Art Club float, 1958. The truck was lent by Gammans & Sons, the coal merchants. The art club still survives today, but not so Gammans & Sons.

A Lancing hospital parade, 14 June 1908. These parades were held every year in the summer long before the NHS was even thought about. All monies collected were for the local hospitals and health care in general. The parades would march through the village up to the manor house grounds, where the lord of the manor, Mr Lloyd, would lay on refreshments. The manor grounds were out of bounds to the villagers except on special occasions like this.

The same parade as above, but a different section. You can clearly see the band and the fire brigade with their brass helmets.

A parade passing the Parish Hall in South Street, Lancing. The reason for this event is not known.

A Lancing and Sompting Royal British Legion parade, North Road, 1932. The women's section was formed in 1929. The ivy-clad cottages are Monks Farm Cottages, with Warren Nurseries next door. The large house at the end was called Warrenhurst. All are now gone and replaced with housing.

May Day, Sompting Abbotts, 1905. The earliest written reference to the Sompting May Day Festival was in a log book from the Church of England National School in 1873. The parade through the village that year collected the grand sum of £2 2s 6d, and each child was given 4d.

The original Marquis of Granby, 22 June 1910. The villagers are celebrating the coronation of King George V.

Section Six

RELIGION

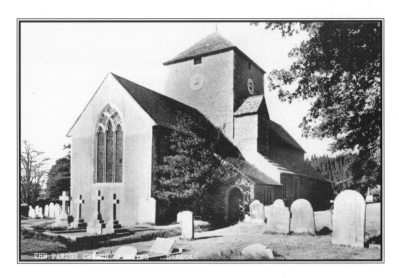

St James the Less, the parish church of Lancing. Situated in the original part of the village, at North Lancing, the church dates back to around 1120. Between 1280 and 1300 the church fabric was almost totally rebuilt in dressed flint with ashlar, except for the stone door mouldings and windows. In August 1969 it was badly damaged by fire. After a lot of work, the church was restored to its former glory.

The Church of St James the Less, in a view looking east towards the chancel, 1916. It is thought that the walls of the chancel date back to Norman times.

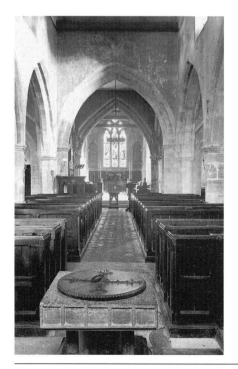

The font, 1917. The font of St James dates back to the twelfth century and is a relic from the original building. It is still in an excellent state of preservation and is used for christenings at the church today.

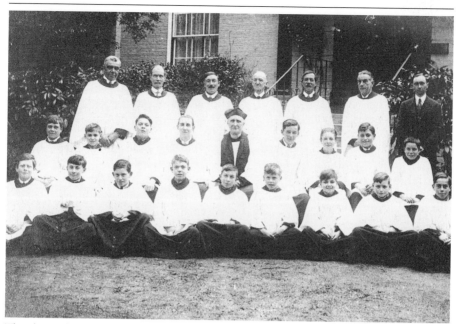

The choir of St James the Less, outside the old vicarage, 1920s.

Sydney Wood, a chorister at the church.
The Wood family came to Lancing in
about 1915 and lived in The Street.
Sydney's father was the village
lamplighter for many years.

Open air service, Vicarage Field, North Lancing, 1935. This event was held to celebrate the silver jubilee of George V.

The old vicarage of St James the Less, pre-1930. The vicarage was built in the early part of the nineteenth century, as its Georgian architecture implies. It was demolished in the 1930s.

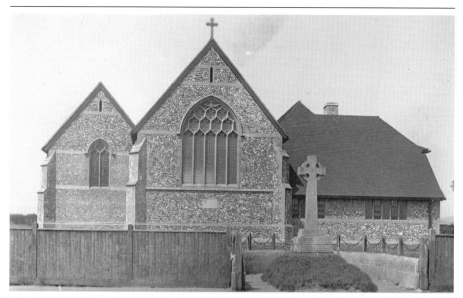

St Michael and All Angels, South Lancing, 1920s. The church in South Street belies its appearance, looking a lot older than it is. It was built in the early 1920s, and dedicated on 5 December 1924. In the foreground is the war memorial, which was later moved to the front of the Parish Hall.

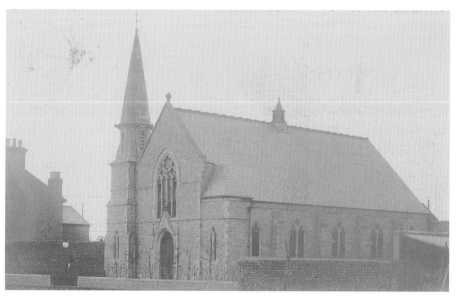

Wesleyan Church, South Street, c. 1909. Built on the site of the old chapel in 1904 by a well-known Worthing building company, Frank Sandells, the chapel cost around £1,800 to build. It is now a Methodist church.

Sompting Parish Church, *c.* 1909. St Mary's was mentioned in the Domesday Book of 1086. In 1154 it was granted to a crusading order of monkish knights, the Templars. The tower is thought to be the only remaining English example of the style known as Rhenish Helm.

Sompting Vicarage, 1908. Largely rebuilt in the nineteenth century, the vicarage remained the residence of the parish priest until 1937. It then became a private house, and was renamed Sompting Peverel.

EDUCATION

The old National School, Mill Road. The school was built in 1872 by subscription and cost about £900. Originally built to take 215 children, it was enlarged at the turn of the century at a further cost of £360. The average attendance was 170 pupils, although during the period of harvest numbers would drop quite dramatically, as the children were required to help in the fields. The school is now the church hall of St James the Less.

Pupils from the National School, 1914. Mr Heaton and Miss Humphries are the teachers.

North Lancing Primary School, 1939. Back row, left to right: Valerie Keemar, Norman Hutchins, Dennis Munnery, -?-, June Schimmel, Dean Francis, -?-, Mary Samson, Keith Woolnough, Dudley Batrick, Ruth Cox. Second row: -?-, Doreen Willard, Celia Bungay, -?-, Margaret Taylor, June Flook, Hilda Atherfold, Len Mortley, Derek Fry. Front row: Peter Giliam, George Kirk, -?-, -?-, Tommy Arnold, Eileen Mills, June Herbert, Hazel Upfield, Pat Gardener, Kathleen Grant. The class teacher was Miss Allman, who later became Mrs Horn. She was still teaching when the author started his school life here in 1964!

North Lancing Primary School pupil Derek Fry, the author's father, *c.* 1937 (see also previous photograph). Mr Fry's links with the school have continued for many years. His own three children were educated there (including the author), and now his three grandchildren attend the school.

Lancing Senior School football team, 1938. Back row, left to right: Les Upton, Mr Sugar, Dick Smith, Roy Prior, Ted Talbot, Tony Lindup, Mr Russel, Rupert Batrick. Front row: Mike Peters, Dudley Davies, G. Green, Tony Groves, Reg Bowles. The school later became Irene Avenue Primary School, and is now called Oakfield Middle School.

Class 1, Sompting National School, *c.* 1915. The master in the photograph is Mr Archard, who later became headmaster at the school. He also ran the football team. The school was built in 1872 at the same time as the North Lancing School. The National School was the primary school of the village until Whitestyles Primary was opened in 1966. The building is now used as a community centre.

The teaching staff at Rectory House, Sompting, when it was a Roman Catholic convent school, 1947. Standing, left to right: Sister Garcia, Mother Mary, Sister Veronica. Seated: Mother Cecelia.

LANCING COLLEGE

AND CHAPEL

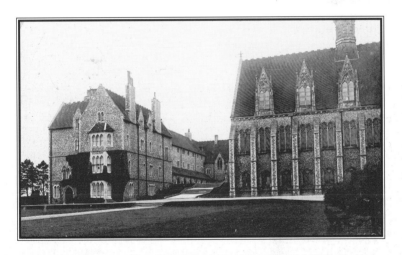

Lancing College, 1911. The college was founded in 1848 by Nathaniel Woodard and is one of twenty schools in the Woodard Foundation. The buildings are made of flint with Caen stone dressing. The first pupils arrived in 1858, three years after the designer, R.H. Carpenter, died.

The college tower, *c.* 1920. The excellent flint work is here for all to see.

The Officers' Training Corps (OTC), *c.* 1914. The cadets are on drill in front of the dining hall. The OTC developed from the cadet corps which began in about 1900. Sometimes as many as three thousand would go through parts of their training at Lancing in the course of a week.

The lower dining hall. This room was built in 1857 and is shown here when it was being used as an armoury.

The old swimming pool. Opened in 1904, the pool was in use until the early 1980s, when it was replaced by a new one.

Lancing College boys on camp at Mytchett, 1913. The sender of this postcard mentions the fact that they had come second in the band competition.

College Farmhouse, with the farm pond in the foreground, *c.* 1920. This postcard was sent as a Christmas greeting.

The first stage of the chapel completed, *c.* 1887. Even to this day, 108 years later, work on the chapel is still unfinished as much of the funds raised have to go towards restoration and repairs, instead of completion works.

The chapel under construction, *c.* 1891. The photograph clearly shows the eastern end (the apse), which was the first part to be completed. Knowing that he would never see the whole structure completed in his lifetime, Woodard had the apse finished first, so that there would be no possibility of the design being cut down in height and changed.

Another view of the chapel apse, 1891. This is how the chapel may have looked when Nathaniel Woodard saw it for the last time, as he died the same year.

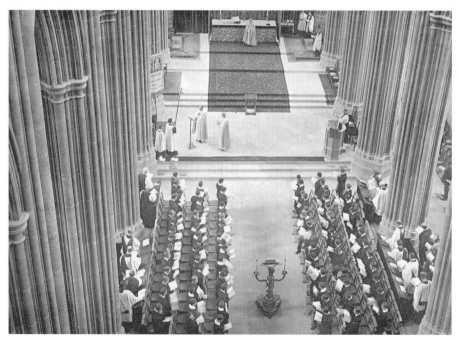

A service taking place in the chapel, *c.* 1914.

The chapel nave, 1904. The floor is being paved with Portland stone. This view shows the Gothic interior at its impressive height of 94 ft. The nave was finished in 1908.

An outstanding building. How Woodard would have loved to have seen the chapel at this stage. The chapel was started in 1868, to the designs of R.H. Carpenter. When the foundations were started, the men found that the ground consisted of clay and sand which was too soft to build on. To find a solid base of chalk they had to dig down, by hand, an average of 60 ft. At the west end of the chapel is a beautiful rose window, the largest of its kind in England.

Section Nine

ORGANIZATION

Lancing Boys' Brigade camp, 1914. In the background is the water tower built by Duke &
Ockendens for the carriage works: the boys are camping just south of it. The aqueduct on
the right carried the water pipe from the tower to the works.

The Rotary Club of Lancing, 1954. This was the year the club was formed and it is still going strong today. The four founder members were Jack Last, John Write, Terence Collier and Bertie Jaques. Behind the group is the rear of the Penstone Hotel, in Penstone Park; this was later demolished.

Victory in Europe party, Lancing and Sompting British Legion Club, Culver Road. The Legion was founded in 1925 (see also p. 49).

St James the Less Youth Club, North Lancing, outside the old National School, *c.* 1946. The group includes, back row, left to right: -?-, Mr Jones, Joan Coles, -?-, -?-, Nancy Muggeridge, -?-, Hazel Upfield, -?-, June Herbert, -?-, -?-, Mr Matthews. Second row: -?-, Diana Knowne, Georgina Grant, Pam Cotton, -?-, Peggy Spencer, Mrs Matthews, Mrs Spencer, -?-, Joyce Avon, Margaret Potts. Front row: Sheila Steele, June Fluke, Polly Matthews, Pat Gardener.

Guildford Fire Brigade finals, 1954. This is the Carriage Works' Brigade in action during an event, using a diesel pump similar to the one used at the works. The firemen are Bill Brown, Bob Burbridge, Johnny Grey and Arthur Webb.

Lancing fire station, South Street. The station house was built in around 1925, replacing the one in North Road. The fire brigade was stationed here for forty-four years until 1969 when it moved to a new station on the Churchill industrial estate. The new station house was a much improved building with better facilities. When opened it had twenty part-time firemen. The old fire station is now an integrated part of the Parish Hall.

Lancing Fire Brigade, *c.* 1945. At this time all the local brigades came under Worthing Rural District Council. The engine seen here had a portable pump which was towed at the rear. An internal pump was fitted in 1954.

THE CARRIAGE WORKS

Staff outside the paint shop, c. 1910. The man with the bowler hat is the foreman, Mr Leppard. Initially the works were just for building and repairing wagon stock. By 1910 they had been developed to include the construction and repair of carriages.

An early view of the Carriage Works, South Lancing. What were the main carriage repair shops in the centre are now part of an industrial unit on the Churchill industrial estate. The white water tower can be seen just beyond the main railway line. The whitewashed cottages in the bottom right were called Dreadnought Cottages. They were one of two pairs of coastguard cottages; the other pair was in front of this one, closer to the Lower Brighton Road.

The wheel shop, *c.* 1910. The wheels made here were wood block wheels. The outer part of the wheel was steel, the inner part wood. This construction was fine for steam trains, but the coming of the electric train saw the demise of the wood block wheel. Electric trains were faster, stopped more often, and braked more fiercely: this caused the outer steel ring to get so hot that it started to char the inner wooden wheel. The works eventually went on to produce all-steel wheels.

The wheel shop, *c.* 1910. The wheels are being manoeuvred out of the shop on tracks to the next stage of construction of the carriage. The small inner track was used to run a trolley truck, which carried the axles waiting to be fitted with wheels.

The wheel shop, *c.* 1910. This area was for machining wheels between centres on a wheel-turning lathe. The wheels were machined to a gauge that had a standard profile for running on the railway track.

The machine and fitting shop, 1912. The men are standing at fitting benches. In the left corner of the photograph are the axle boxes, which were placed at the end of the axle on the wheels.

The smiths' shop, 1912. One of the many items the blacksmiths made was something called a three-linked welded coupling, for the coupling of carriages. Ike Pilot, the man in the foreground, was the foreman. He pioneered a method of producing this coupling with one single weld, instead of three.

The tool room enclosure, 1936. This was an integral part of the wheel shop. Left side, front to back: Hubert Marshall, Harry Beales, Lesley Pearce, Jack Ralph. Right side, front to back: -?-, Albert Pearce, Ernest Steele, Ted Marchant. The man in the centre was the charge man, Art Sensier.

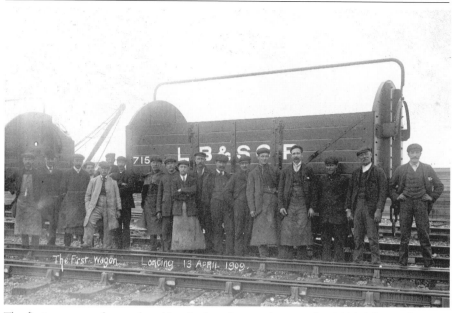

The first wagon to be produced by the Lancing carriage works, 1909. The works were part of the London, Brighton and South Coast Railway Company. The man with the bowler hat, standing second from the left, would most definitely be the foreman.

One of the many different trucks that were made at the works. This is a gunpowder truck which would have been used by the mining industry.

A match truck made at the works, 1914. These were used in conjunction with a travelling rail crane. The long jib of the crane would rest in between the two upright poles, then be secured with the chain.

A two-car electric, fitted with an experimental rubber suspension. This idea was never developed because of the cost.

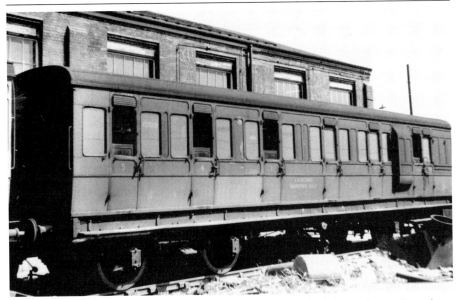

Part of The Lancing Belle, the Carriage Works' train which brought workers from Brighton to Lancing. The Belle was first introduced in 1919.

A catering trolley for use on railway station platforms, 1957. It was one of the more unusual items made at the works.

The memorial to all the men from the works who lost their lives in the First World War. The memorial was situated at the south entrance to the works. It is still there, but now stands in a car park on the Churchill industrial estate. The inscribed tablets have been transferred to the village war memorial outside the Parish Hall.

Lancing Carriage Works' Fire Brigade, 1938. Back row, left to right: Mr Conley, Mr Meads, Mr Warr, Mr Bradbury, Mr Amos, Mr Richardson. Front row: Mr Bobbing, Mr Hayes, Mr Hunt, Mr Dunn, Mr Mansfield. The brigade was run on a totally voluntary basis.

Lancing Carriage Works' Fire Brigade, 1952. Left to right: Jock Potter, Bill Brown, Johnny Grey, Gunner Dixon, Mr Collins (works' manager), Arthur Webb, Norman McCiver, Bob Burbridge. The brigade had a successful year at the annual fire brigade competition at Guildford (see p. 93).

Carriage Works' Military Band, *c.* 1920. The works had a few bands, one of which was a silver band that used to play when the men collected their wages.

Section Eleven

WAR

No. 3 Platoon, Lancing A Company, 9th Battery Sussex Home Guard, December 1944.
Under the command of Lieutenant Robinson and 2nd Lieutenant Wilmshurst the Home
Guard used to meet at South Lancing Primary School (now Freshbrook School) in North
Road. This group includes Mr Mott, Mr Hounsell, Mr Cotton, Charlie Hunniball,
Jack Upfield, Mr Seddon, Bob Macguiness, Mr Barnes, Hedley Wilmshurst,
Mr Robinson, Sid Parfitt, Mr Lillywhite, Bob Walker.

Another section of the Home Guard. These are all members of the Lancing and Sompting Royal British Legion. They are collected outside the club in Culver Road.

A 'Salute the Soldier' parade marching up South Street towards the railway crossing, 13 May 1944.

Damage to Sompting Primary School, 1941. Both Lancing and Sompting lay within the notorious strip which was named 'Bomb Alley' during the Second World War. This was the area from the coast to London, which was frequently bombed.

A street party, First Avenue, Lancing, May 1945. This was held on VE Day to celebrate the end of the Second World War in Europe. Some of the people involved include members of the Fry family, Eveline, Elva, Albert, Eddie, Ray and Derek, and members of the Green family, Bet, Margaret, Bob and Jim. Also present are Jackie Jasper, Graham Law, Nancy Palmer, Arthur and Vera Puckett, Mrs Reynolds and Maureen Reynolds, Mrs Berry and Dennis Berry, Mamey Bowden, Mrs Symonds and Mick Symonds, and Rolly Elliot. It was a time when the avenues still had trees!

Remembrance Day service, the war memorial, South Street, South Lancing, early 1930s. With standards lowered in salute, members of Lancing and Sompting British Legion remember the dead of the First World War.

Lancing war memorial, c. 1925. The memorial was erected in the grounds of St Michael's Church in South Street. It was later moved a few yards along the street to the grounds of the Parish Hall.

Section Twelve

DISASTERS

Fairhaven, 1913. This was one of the many bungalows at Bungalow Town totally destroyed by the Easter storm on 23 March 1913. Fairhaven belonged to a renowned Victorian strongman called Hackenschmidt. He was of German, Swedish and Russian descent. His trainer used to have to carry him into the sea, as Hackenschmidt complained that the pebbles hurt his feet!

The Easter storm, 23 March 1913. This was the first in a series of postcards made from photographs taken by the McArthy brothers.

This photograph shows the full extent of the damage caused by the storm. The bungalows here have been shifted up the beach, and have disintegrated.

The severity of the storm was such that part of the pier at Worthing was washed away. There was no hope for this bungalow.

Fire at Yew Tree Cottages, August 1957. This row of six thatched cottages was in South Street at the junction with Penhill Road (see p. 13). The fire started at the northern end of the row. The thatched roofs enabled the fire to take hold quickly and the cottages were destroyed.

A fireman directing his hose at what is left of Yew Tree Cottages. During the fire one of the Lancing trailer pumps broke down when the cooling tank overheated and exploded.

The aftermath of a fire at Sussex Pad, North Lancing, 1905. The fire occurred on the night of 25 October 1905. It is said to have started in the kitchen chimney, and then spread to some of the old beams. All that was left was smouldering ruins; yet another piece of old Lancing disappears.

Section Thirteen

VILLAGE PEOPLE

The Fry family, c. 1940. Family members shown are Frank and Eveline (Eve), with their

children Cyril, Derek ('Snakey'), Elva, Grace, Albert ('Biggy'), Ray, Eddie, Pat and Rita.

The family came to Lancing in 1931. Albert Fry Snr, father of Frank, had his own

building company, A.E. Fry. Along with another company, owned by Paddy Moxom, they

developed the avenues: Orchard, First, Second, etc. The family lived in Church Path (now

First Avenue), which they also built. Both Cyril and Albert ('Biggy') went on to have their

own building companies in Lancing. Cyril also had a builders merchant's shop in Crabtree

Lane. A large number of family members still live in Lancing and Sompting, some 64 years

on!

Albert Cosham, *c*. 1920. Mr Cosham is shown in his Automobile Association uniform. He was a Special Constable in Lancing during the war years. He lived in Church Path.

Mr Henry Howells in the meadow next to The Haven on the Lower Brighton Road, Lancing, where he lived. Mr Howells was a well-to-do gentleman who owned a draper's shop in Pimlico, London, as well as having nurseries in Lancing for fruit growing.

Mr and Mrs Charles Burtenshaw in their cottage garden at 33 North Road, *c.* 1911. Mr Burtenshaw was a farm hand at Culver Farm, Lancing.

Hazel Upfield (now Trussler), Grinstead Lane, 1932. Hazel is standing outside Grinstead Cottages, one of which was her home. Her father, Jack, was a market gardener at North Lancing. Note the perambulator.

Jim Wood lived in The Street, North Lancing, and was at one time the village lamplighter. He later became caretaker at North Lancing Primary School.

The village fire brigade, 1920s. The brigade was organized by J.H. Greet. A hand cart and hose were provided by donations from parishioners.

The staff of Sompting Abbotts, 1913. The man with the dog and the rifle is the gamekeeper. The donkey can also be seen in the photograph of the Abbotts on p. 18.

The Coleman family from Sompting, 1917. Left to right: Fred, Jim, Fred Jnr, Ernest, Jane, with Tom in the centre front. Like a lot of local people Fred junior, Ernest and Tom all worked at Pullen-Burry's nurseries.

Latimer Cottages, West Street, Sompting, 1917. Jane Coleman and Frank Firmin stand outside Jane Coleman's home. At this time Frank Firmin was churchwarden at St Mary's. He lived at Stocks House, West Street.

George Humphrey from Sompting, a shepherd who worked on Lambley's Farm, Lambley's Lane, which is situated on the Sompting and Broadwater border.

Jack Beacher, Titch Hill, 1937. Mr Beacher was a Sompting shepherd, who lived at Danton Cottages. He worked for Ernie Wadman, who owned Yew Tree Farm.

Section Fourteen

PUBLIC HOUSES

The Sussex Pad, North Lancing, pre-1905. Dating back to the fifteenth century, this was

the oldest pub in the village but was destroyed by fire in 1905. It was frequented by many

a smuggler during the eighteenth and nineteenth centuries. As the pub was situated near the

banks of the River Adur, it was a convenient spot from which to transport contraband up

river. The name 'pad' seems to be associated with the pack-horses of yesteryear.

The new Sussex Pad, shown here *c.* 1945, was built in 1906 to replace the original.

The Corner House, North Lancing, *c.* 1937. Now called the Sussex Potter, this pub was built on the old Brighton Road (now Manor Road) in the early 1930s to serve people living in the steadily expanding housing development in North Lancing. The sender of the postcard felt it was quite important to mention that 'the man who lives in this house has a television set'!

The Three Horseshoes, which dates back to around 1807. Being so isolated and close to the sea this pub was popular with smugglers. In 1896 the barque *Ophir* was caught in a storm and beached off South Lancing. It was arranged for the captain and his crew to stay at the 'Shoes to recover. The crew were so grateful to the landlord, a Mr Prideaux, that they presented him with a goat! The pub still exists, at the bottom of South Street, minus one goat.

The Railway Hotel and the level crossing, Lancing, in a view looking north, early 1900s. The hotel was built in 1870 and was renamed the Merry Monk in 1973.

The junction of Busticle Lane and West Street, Sompting, 1904. The white building on the right of the photograph was a beer retailer known as The Ball, although locals called it Aunt Annie's. The Balltree Pub now stands in its place.

The old Marquis of Granby, 1926. This building dated back to the beginning of the nineteenth century. It was demolished in the 1930s and replaced by a new pub which kept the same name.

Section Fifteen

ROADS

South Street, South Lancing, under snow, 1908. The small shop with the canopy is the Lancing Dairy, which at this time was run by Walter Grover.

The Lower Brighton Road, in a view looking east, 1924. At one time a toll-house stood at both the Worthing end and the Shoreham end.

Kings Road, South Lancing, in a view looking north, *c.* 1930. Up to the late 1920s half of the road leading from South Street was known as Farmers' Lane. When the farmers had finished for the day they used to walk up the lane and congregate in a building where the Farmers' Hotel now stands. This is most probably how the pub got its name.

Kings Road, in a view looking south, *c.* 1921. This is roughly where Farmers' Lane used to end.

Queens Road, in a view looking north, early 1930s.

Penhill Road, in a view looking east, early 1900s. One of the oldest roads in Lancing, Penhill Road was called Jubilee Road when it opened in 1887. There was a brickworks here, which used local clay, an industry now long gone in Lancing.

Sompting Road where it meets Boundstone Lane, *c.* 1925. This is the western boundary between Lancing and Sompting.

North Road, Lancing, in a view looking south towards the railway crossing, 1908. The shops shown here were the only ones in North Road at this time and consisted of a grocer's (Ernest Palmer), the post office (where Arthur Bartlett was the sub-postmaster), a butcher's (David Snelling), a bootmaker's (Henry Peters), and a confectioner's (Martha Wiseman).

First Avenue, c. 1935. At this time Second Avenue was actually part of First Avenue. The southern end of First Avenue was blocked by an old flint wall: this was later removed.

Local builder, Bob Steele, laying the road in his steam roller, 1948. He is at the top of Hamilton Road, at the junction with Greet Road.

West Lane, North Lancing, in a view looking north, 1925. At one time the lane ran unbroken from St James the Less all the way down into South Lancing.

The Street, *c.* 1920. This was the main thoroughfare through the original part of the village at North Lancing, and dates back to the time of the Domesday Book in 1086. Most of the houses at this end of The Street are still standing and are now part of a designated conservation area.

The old Brighton Road (now Manor Road), North Lancing, *c.* 1910. The view looks towards the Old Cottage with the aptly named Corner House on the left. The Corner House was built in the eighteenth century. (Both these buildings are referred to in earlier sections.) The children are from the primary school, next to the Old Cottage.

Mill Road, North Lancing, in a view looking north, *c*. 1910. The road takes its name from the post windmill that stood on The Downs, in the area of the chalk pit. One of the millers at the mill in the eighteenth century was John Olliver, now famous as the occupant of the 'miller's tomb' at Highdown, in Goring, Sussex. The mill was demolished in 1905.

West Street, Sompting, in a view looking west, 1922. This was the main thoroughfare through Sompting at the time.

THE SOUTHERN CONVALESCENT HOMES

Hope Lodge was built in 1896 for underprivileged mothers and children. It was one of many homes William Chorley had in South Lancing. His headquarters were the North East London Gospel Mission in Grosvenor Road, Canonbury, which he started in 1885. The homes in South Lancing came under the heading of the Southern Convalescent Homes and were formed in 1890. Most of the inmates of the homes came from London. Hope Lodge was in South Street, a few yards north of the Three Horseshoes pub: the lodge was later demolished.

Mothers and children at Hope Lodge, 1909. Note the galvanized buckets and spades.

Chestnuts, South Street, *c*. 1906. The original part of this building was at one time the Lancing Grammar School, built in around 1820. When the school closed in around 1890, Mr Chorley acquired the premises rent-free, but only if it was used as a women's convalescent home, which it duly became. The home was demolished in the early 1930s to make way for a parade of shops on the corner of South Street and the Lower Brighton Road.

The occupants of Chestnuts, 1909. On the right of the group the name of Tamplins brewery is visible through the trees. This was displayed on the front of the Three Horseshoes pub.

Another group at Chestnuts, 1911. The sender of this postcard is in the photograph. These photographs were normally taken before patients went home after recovering. By this time the home was taking in children as well.

The dining room at Chestnuts, 1908.

The Bell Memorial Home, *c.* 1920. This home was for women; on its left was the Sunbeam Home for Children. The two homes are now incorporated into one rest home. The building is 104 years old and is situated near the bottom of South Street.

Channel View patients, 1908. This home was opened in 1899 and was originally for men with chest problems. It was soon catering for convalescing women as well. The men were known to the villagers as 'Chorleys Blue Birds' because of their uniforms of navy blue suits. The home was on the Lower Brighton Road.

Channel View patients, this time with some of the staff, 1909.

Channel View, *c.* 1922. At this time the home was catering for convalescing women only. The home was later demolished to make way for housing.

Beachville, *c.* 1920. Another of Chorley's homes, Beachville was situated on the Lower Brighton Road. It was bought by the West Sussex County Council, which, in 1957, re-named it Sussex Lodge, as it is still known today. It is now a rest home for both men and women.

Patients of Beachville, 1915. The local nurserymen must have done a brisk trade when these group photographs were taken, as nearly everyone has a buttonhole!

The smoking room at Beachville, 1920s.

Mount Hermon was built in 1907 on the Lower Brighton Road. Originally it was for the 'aged and dying'. The building still exists today as a rest home.

Mount Hermon patients, 1909. The lady in the front row couldn't sit still long enough for the long exposure time required, and has ended up with a blurred face.

RURAL LIFE AND NURSERIES

William Phillips Jnr, North Road, Lancing. Mr Phillips was a son of the owner of Monks Farm, who was also one of the first parish councillors of Lancing. E. Phillips, another son, owned Church Farm on Church Lane, Sompting. The Phillipses came from the West Country and the locals often misunderstood them because of their accent!

Fuller's nursery, 1909. Like most of the crops in Lancing and Sompting, grapes grew well in the area because of the mild climate. Fuller had nurseries in the areas of Sompting Road and Penhill Road. Houses have now been built on both sites.

Vinery, one of Fuller's nurseries, *c.* 1910.

Railway Hotel, North Road, Lancing, *c.* 1910. Note all the trees in North Road.

North Road, in a view looking north. Culver Farmhouse is to the left, with Littlecroft to the right (see p. 13). This whole area is now covered in shops, making it hard to believe that this rural scene ever existed in Lancing.

Old Cottages, North Road, Lancing, 1908. These cottages are situated in the area of North Farm Road. The gable end of the cottages can be seen in the previous photograph, to the right of the trees. Mr Green is coming out of his cottage.

A view across the harvest fields from Lancing to The Downs, *c.* 1922. Lancing Clump looks splendid on the brow of the Downs. Unfortunately it was completely devastated during the storm of 1987.

A greenhouse full of chrysanthemums belonging to the Crabtree Nurseries, Lancing. These would have been sent to Covent Garden by train.

Staff of Malthouse Nursery, 1920s. The nursery was to the east of Grinstead Lane, Lancing.

Nash Brothers of Lancing, whose market garden industry was in the Mash Barn area, *c*. 1906. They had their own tokens which were used as receipts for deposits on the empty containers used for their produce. The containers can be seen here on the wagon.

John Upfield (Jack), *c*. 1948. Mr Upfield is standing in the 'big field' at Malthouse Nursery, North Lancing. This area is now the Leisure Centre car park.

Making a hay rick in the area around Hoe Court Farm, North Lancing, early 1930s. Note the fine Sussex wagon.

The village smithy, Mill Road, North Lancing, 1908. The blacksmith at this time was John Broomfield. The thatched building is the old Granary. The splendid walnut tree in the centre is in the garden of the aptly named Walnut Tree Cottage.

Hill Barn Farm, North Lancing, 1958. Lancing College and Chapel are in the distance. This view will disappear if plans for the A27 Worthing/Lancing road 'improvement' get the go-ahead.

Shepherd William Hurst and his dog in Sixteen Acre Field, Hoe Court Farm, North Lancing. The buildings of the farm are in the background.

Lancing Clump, 1926. A rather demure-looking young lady poses in the quite dense woodland. Locals still enjoy walking here, although there are fewer trees.

The inside of one of Pullen-Burry's moving greenhouses. One of the wheels can be seen sitting on the track, which was made up of bricks laid on edge. The greenhouse was manoeuvred by hand over the crops when they needed to be brought on quicker.

Sompting Nurseries, 1918. Fred and Tom Coleman of Latimer Terrace, West Street, are standing among the chrysanthemums.

The village smithy, West Street, Sompting, 1904. William Weller is the blacksmith. The smithy is now a private house.

BRITAIN IN OLD PHOTOGRAPHS

To order any of these titles please telephone Littlehampton Book Services on 01903 721596

ALDERNEY

Alderney: A Second Selection, *B Bonnard*

BEDFORDSHIRE

Bedfordshire at Work, *N Lutt*

BERKSHIRE

Maidenhead, *M Hayles & D Hedges*
Around Maidenhead, *M Hayles & B Hedges*
Reading, *P Southerton*
Reading: A Second Selection, *P Southerton*
Sandhurst and Crowthorne, *K Dancy*
Around Slough, *J Hunter & K Hunter*
Around Thatcham, *P Allen*
Around Windsor, *B Hedges*

BUCKINGHAMSHIRE

Buckingham and District, *R Cook*
High Wycombe, *R Goodearl*
Around Stony Stratford, *A Lambert*

CHESHIRE

Cheshire Railways, *M Hitches*
Chester, *S Nichols*

CLWYD

Clwyd Railways, *M Hitches*

CLYDESDALE

Clydesdale, *Lesmahagow Parish Historical Association*

CORNWALL

Cornish Coast, *T Bowden*
Falmouth, *P Gilson*
Lower Fal, *P Gilson*
Around Padstow, *M McCarthy*
Around Penzance, *J Holmes*
Penzance and Newlyn, *J Holmes*
Around Truro, *A Lyne*
Upper Fal, *P Gilson*

CUMBERLAND

Cockermouth and District, *J Bernard Bradbury*
Keswick and the Central Lakes, *J Marsh*
Around Penrith, *F Boyd*
Around Whitehaven, *H Fancy*

DERBYSHIRE

Derby, *D Buxton*
Around Matlock, *D Barton*

DEVON

Colyton and Seaton, *T Gosling*
Dawlish and Teignmouth, *G Gosling*
Devon Aerodromes, *K Saunders*
Exeter, *P Thomas*
Exmouth and Budleigh Salterton, *T Gosling*
From Haldon to Mid-Dartmoor, *T Hall*
Honiton and the Otter Valley, *J Yallop*
Around Kingsbridge, *K Tanner*
Around Seaton and Sidmouth, *T Gosling*
Seaton, Axminster and Lyme Regis, *T Gosling*

DORSET

Around Blandford Forum, *B Cox*
Bournemouth, *M Colman*
Bridport and the Bride Valley, *J Burrell & S Humphries*
Dorchester, *T Gosling*
Around Gillingham, *P Crocker*

DURHAM

Darlington, *G Flynn*
Darlington: A Second Selection, *G Flynn*
Durham People, *M Richardson*
Houghton-le-Spring and Hetton-le-Hole, *K Richardson*
Houghton-le-Spring and Hetton-le-Hole:
  A Second Selection, *K Richardson*
Sunderland, *S Miller & B Bell*
Teesdale, *D Coggins*
Teesdale: A Second Selection, *P Raine*
Weardale, *J Crosby*
Weardale: A Second Selection, *J Crosby*

DYFED

Aberystwyth and North Ceredigion,
  Dyfed Cultural Services Dept
Haverfordwest, *Dyfed Cultural Services Dept*
Upper Tywi Valley, *Dyfed Cultural Services Dept*

ESSEX

Around Grays, *B Evans*

GLOUCESTERSHIRE

Along the Avon from Stratford to Tewkesbury, *J Jeremiah*
Cheltenham: A Second Selection, *R Whiting*
Cheltenham at War, *P Gill*
Cirencester, *J Welsford*
Around Cirencester, *E Cuss & P Griffiths*
Forest, The, *D Mullin*
Gloucester, *J Voyce*
Around Gloucester, *A Sutton*
Gloucester: From the Walwin Collection, *J Voyce*
North Cotswolds, *D Viner*
Severn Vale, *A Sutton*
Stonehouse to Painswick, *A Sutton*
Stroud and the Five Valleys, *S Gardiner & L Padin*
Stroud and the Five Valleys: A Second Selection,
  S Gardiner & L Padin
Stroud's Golden Valley, *S Gardiner & L Padin*
Stroudwater and Thames & Severn Canals,
  E Cuss & S Gardiner
Stroudwater and Thames & Severn Canals: A Second
  Selection, *E Cuss & S Gardiner*
Tewkesbury and the Vale of Gloucester, *C Hilton*
Thornbury to Berkeley, *J Hudson*
Uley, Dursley and Cam, *A Sutton*
Wotton-under-Edge to Chipping Sodbury, *A Sutton*

GWYNEDD

Anglesey, *M Hitches*
Gwynedd Railways, *M Hitches*
Around Llandudno, *M Hitches*
Vale of Conwy, *M Hitches*

HAMPSHIRE

Gosport, *J Sadden*
Portsmouth, *P Rogers & D Francis*

HEREFORDSHIRE

Herefordshire, *A Sandford*

HERTFORDSHIRE

Barnet, *I Norrie*
Hitchin, *A Fleck*
St Albans, *S Mullins*
Stevenage, *M Appleton*

ISLE OF MAN

The Tourist Trophy, *B Snelling*

ISLE OF WIGHT

Newport, *D Parr*
Around Ryde, *D Parr*

JERSEY

Jersey: A Third Selection, *R Lemprière*

KENT

Bexley, *M Scott*
Broadstairs and St Peter's, *J Whyman*
Bromley, Keston and Hayes, *M Scott*
Canterbury: A Second Selection, *D Butler*
Chatham and Gillingham, *P MacDougall*
Chatham Dockyard, *P MacDougall*
Deal, *J Broady*
Early Broadstairs and St Peter's, *B Wootton*
East Kent at War, *D Collyer*
Eltham, *J Kennett*
Folkestone: A Second Selection, *A Taylor & E Rooney*
Goudhurst to Tenterden, *A Guilmant*
Gravesend, *R Hiscock*
Around Gravesham, *R Hiscock & D Grierson*
Herne Bay, *J Hawkins*
Lympne Airport, *D Collyer*
Maidstone, *I Hales*
Margate, *R Clements*
RAF Hawkinge, *R Humphreys*
RAF Manston, *RAF Manston History Club*
RAF Manston: A Second Selection,
  RAF Manston History Club
Ramsgate and Thanet Life, *D Perkins*
Romney Marsh, *E Carpenter*
Sandwich, *C Wanostrocht*
Around Tonbridge, *C Bell*
Tunbridge Wells, *M Rowlands & I Beavis*
Tunbridge Wells: A Second Selection,
  M Rowlands & I Beavis
Around Whitstable, *C Court*
Wingham, Adisham and Littlebourne, *M Crane*

LANCASHIRE

Around Barrow-in-Furness, *J Garbutt & J Marsh*
Blackpool, *C Rothwell*
Bury, *J Hudson*
Chorley and District, *J Smith*
Fleetwood, *C Rothwell*
Heywood, *J Hudson*
Around Kirkham, *C Rothwell*
Lancashire North of the Sands, *J Garbutt & J Marsh*
Around Lancaster, *S Ashworth*
Lytham St Anne's, *C Rothwell*
North Fylde, *C Rothwell*
Radcliffe, *J Hudson*
Rossendale, *B Moore & N Dunnachie*

LEICESTERSHIRE

Around Ashby-de-la-Zouch, *K Hillier*
Charnwood Forest, *I Keil, W Humphrey & D Wix*
Leicester, *D Burton*
Leicester: A Second Selection, *D Burton*
Melton Mowbray, *T Hickman*
Around Melton Mowbray, *T Hickman*
River Soar, *D Wix, P Shacklock & I Keil*
Rutland, *T Clough*
Vale of Belvoir, *T Hickman*
Around the Welland Valley, *S Mastoris*

LINCOLNSHIRE

Grimsby, *J Tierney*
Around Grimsby, *J Tierney*
Grimsby Docks, *J Tierney*
Lincoln, *D Cuppleditch*